TABLE FOR TWO

MAKING A GOOD MARRIAGE
BETTER

TABLE FOR TWO

Avraham Peretz Friedman

TARGUM/FELDHEIM

First published 1992

Copyright © 1992 by Cary Friedman
ISBN 0-944070-98-1 Softcover

Phototypeset at Targum Press

Published by:
Targum Press Inc.
22700 W. Eleven Mile Rd.
Southfield, Mich. 48034

Distributed by:
Feldheim Publishers
200 Airport Executive Park
Spring Valley, N.Y. 10977

Distributed in Israel by:
Nof Books Ltd.
POB 43170
Jerusalem 91430

Printed in Israel

IN MEMORY

OF

MY BELOVED GRANDPARENTS
ISAAK BARAN AND
IDA SHOAG BARAN

AND

MY DEAR UNCLE
WARREN SHOAG-BARAN

DEDICATION

To MARSHA,
MY WIFE AND BEST FRIEND

ACKNOWLEDGMENTS

SEVERAL PEOPLE CONTRIBUTED to the production of this book, and I am glad to thank them publicly: Joan Joyette, Avi Leiter, and B. Siegfried.

It has been my great privilege to learn from many outstanding teachers and models of Torah. I humbly acknowledge my gratitude to the following Rebbeim:

HaRav HaGaon Avigdor Miller, *shlita*

R. Yehudah Parnes, *shlita*

R. Yitzchak Shurin, *shlita*

R. Mordechai Tendler, *shlita*

R. Shaya Karlinsky, *shlita*

R. Yaakov Bulua, *shlita*

R. Moshe Goldberger, *shlita*

Special thanks to R. Daniel Arm, *shlita*, who has been both my rebbe and my friend, and exemplifies the finest qualities of both careers.

My heartfelt thanks to my parents-in-law, Robert and Evelyn Harris, for providing us with a fine model of a Jewish home. May Hashem bless them with long life, good health, happiness, and *nachas* from their children and grandchildren.

My deepest gratitude to my parents, Edward and Esia Friedman, for all they have done — and continue to do — for us. They have been a source of constant inspiration and encouragement over the years. I pray the *Ribono shel Olam* rewards their selfless devotion to their family with long life, good health, happiness, and *nachas* from their children and grandchildren.

In her humble, unassuming way, my wife, Marsha, embodies and animates the profound *mussar* ideals depicted in this book. May we share many more years together, in happiness and health, enjoying *nachas* from our wonderful children, Elisha, Devora Adina, and Ayelet.

CONTENTS

PREFACE

MOST COMPLEX EQUIPMENT comes with an operator's instruction manual. Marriage is far more complex and sophisticated than just about anything else on the market. However, we are expected to figure out on our own how to make it work. This book attempts to ease that process by giving some of the invaluable wisdom of our Torah and its Sages. The book you are holding in your hands was designed to be a practical handbook for improving your marriage — and in the process, yourself.

Even a good marriage can benefit from some further improvement. If you already have a good marriage, great. Thank God. Now make it even better. The difference between a good marriage and a great one is like the difference between being not sick and being truly healthy. A person who is not sick is, admittedly, not racked with pain or illness, *b"H.* But that's a far cry from being healthy, from experiencing the exuberance and buoyancy of being really physically fit, of possessing a physique that works smoothly and efficiently, with everything (all bodily systems) in harmony. Lack of illness is fundamentally different from robust energy and enthusiasm. The same distinction applies to marriage.

Though this book was designed to be as general as possible, clearly it is not for everyone and every situation. These rules and the philosophy that underlies them presuppose two basically normal, if at times intractable, marriage partners. If this describes your situation, then the advice in this book may be useful for you. In any event, before you decide that the advice given here is not for you and that you are one of those few, exceptional cases, try it and see if it works. Whatever you do, don't make the tragic error of condemning hastily or lightly a marriage that is, in its essence, a viable one. Even the most unhappy marriages are usually capable of improvement and correction.

A day or two before I got married, a well-meaning relative said he wished to share with me the secret of being a good husband and having a happy marriage. "But", he concluded in mock despair, "God only knows how to do that." He was right. Without knowing it or meaning to, he gave me the most significant piece of advice he — or anyone — could have given: God does know how we should live life successfully, and He taught us how in His *Torat Chayim* (lit., "instructions for living").

Sometimes, just knowing that something is possible is itself liberating. The story is told that Mozart once wrote a violin concerto that was so intricate and demanding that it was believed to be physically unplayable (because of the structure of the hand). Mozart entreated one celebrated violinist after another, but each one, convinced that it could not be played, declined. Later that same year, a hitherto unknown violinist shocked his audience and the musical world by successfully playing Mozart's composition. Within a short time, there were many performances of the piece that had earlier been dismissed as unplayable.

What had happened to those violinists who had once been so skeptical? Did the structure of their hands change since they had first refused Mozart's entreaties? No, of course not. They had seen it done, or, rather, they now knew it could be done. So, too, the ambitious goal discussed in this book. This book portrays a high level of marital trust and teamwork. Know that it *can* be done, it *can* be attained.

Pursue this worthwhile goal with unflagging enthusiasm and diligence, and you will surely, *iy"H*, be rewarded for your efforts.

A quick survey of the rules given in this book will reveal that there is nothing exotic, revolutionary, bizarre, or unduly hard about them. The benefit to be had from these sensible suggestions comes from their constant, consistent application.

With great power comes great responsibility. The

Almighty has given each of us power in variegated forms. For example, a husband and wife are given the enormous power to create (in "partnership" with the Almighty) a human being, and with that power comes the equally enormous responsibility to physically care for and raise the child to be a moral and ethical human being. This is a particularly dramatic example, but the lesson is as true and applicable in any of the other arenas in which we play out our lives. Every role we play (as parents, children, friends, neighbors, coworkers, etc.), every part the Creator has cast us in, endows us with tremendous, staggering powers, and He watches to see that we exercise these cosmic gifts with the appropriate responsibility.

A husband and wife are each given awesome powers from the moment they leave the *chupah*, and responsibilities — sobering responsibilities — to match.

Good luck!

1
INTRODUCTION

> "All the affairs of the world...are *nisyonot*
> [trials] for a person" (*Mesilat Yesharim*, ch. 1).

AS R. MOSHE CHAIM LUZZATO, author of the *mussar* classic *Mesilat Yesharim*, observed, everything in life — every incident, episode, and encounter — is a *nisayon*.

What is a *nisayon*? And why does the Almighty provide us with an endless continuum of them?

A *nisayon* is an opportunity for — and an invitation to — greatness. The Almighty sends *nisyonot* to a person in order to spiritually elevate him or her. The Ramban explains:

> The Almighty gives a person a *nisayon* in order to...draw out the actual from the po-

tential, so that the person can receive a
reward for doing a good deed, and not just
a reward for having a good inclination....[1]

A *nisayon* provides an opportunity and the motivation for a person to tap into and use the many strengths
the Creator gave him. Rather than allow those enormous
God-given potentials to remain dormant, the Almighty
sends a person *nisyonot* to encourage him to actualize
them to a degree heretofore unattained, perhaps even
unimagined. The greater the *nisayon*, the greater the
impetus for personal growth and refinement of character.
Nisyonot are essential if we are to succeed in our mission
in life.

It should be noted that a *nisayon* may be challenging
and demanding, but it need not be unpleasant. Indeed,
sometimes the occasions of the greatest happiness fur-
nish the most profound *nisyonot*.

The institution of marriage is one of the greatest
nisyonot a person will be blessed with in his or her life.

The Midrash relates that Elkanah, the father of Shmuel
Hanavi, was the greatest person of his generation. It was
this greatness that enabled him to singlehandedly restore
the phenomenon of *aliyah leregel* to Shiloh to its former
magnificence and splendor.

How did he attain this greatness?

The verse says, *"Ve'alah ha'ish ha'hu mei'iro,"*[2] —

---

1. Bereishit 22:1.
2. Shmuel I 1:3.

and this man [Elkanah] went up from his city. The Midrash elaborates on the phrase *"ve'alah"*: Elkanah "went up" in spiritual greatness as well. "He became great *bevaito* [in his *bayit*]; he became great in his neighborhood; he became great in his city; ultimately, he became great in all of Israel."[3]

The message is clear. The beginning of a career of greatness — of service to the Almighty — begins *"bevaito,"* with a person's *bayit*.

What is a person's *bayit*?

The Gemara supplies the last piece of the puzzle:

> "R. Yose said, 'I never called my wife "my wife"; I only called her "my *bayit*" [my home]' " (*Shabbat* 118b).

> " '...And the kohen shall atone for himself and for his *bayit* [home]' [Vayikra 16:6] — 'Home' refers to his wife" (*Yoma* 13a).

Marriage is the most intense, concentrated process possible for improving our personal characteristics — our *middot*. That is our primary mission in life, the reason for our very existence in this world. That is the essence of *avodat Hashem* (service of God).[4] This improvement can only happen through our relationships to people. After all, it doesn't take much effort to be a tzaddik, and have good (even great) *middot*, when no one else is

---

3. *Bemidbar Rabbah* 10:12
4. Vilna Gaon, *Even Sheleimah* 1:1,2.

around. There is no temptation — because there is no opportunity — to speak *lashon hara*. There is no stirring of jealousy and no clamoring for honor. The improvement of bad *middot* is only possible when there is interaction with other people. And that is what the Almighty wants: He wants us to work hard — to struggle, in fact — and triumph in the process of self-perfection.

Marriage is the arena ideally suited for this process. In marriage, perfecting one's character — *tikun hamiddot* — can occur to an unparalleled degree.

The institution of marriage has the uncanny ability, like nothing else, to transform *everything* you do into a mitzvah.

Before you were married, the Master of the Universe didn't particularly care if you bought regular or "home-style" orange juice (with little pieces of pulp in it). Suppose you liked home-style, *ess gezunter hait.* That was, essentially, a "neutral" choice, outside the sphere of mitzvot. After you married a wonderful woman who happens to hate little pieces of orange pulp in her juice, however, your decision regarding which kind of orange juice to buy when you go shopping takes on profound, new significance. Shopping becomes a spectacular opportunity for acquiring and demonstrating consideration and selflessness, or, *ch"v,* a dismal exercise in selfishness and inconsideration. Funny as it may sound, passing up the home-style orange juice (your choice) in favor of the regular variety (because it is your wife's choice) has made you a greater man.

Once upon a time, perhaps, you squeezed the toothpaste tube wherever you felt like it, satisfied that something always came out. Or you put the cereal box back into the cabinet with 1/16 of a teaspoon of cereal left kicking around in it — and no one cared. Now, though, your husband — justified or not — has his shtick: he doesn't like it. In fact, it makes him crazy. Today, you gingerly roll the tube up from the bottom, or toss the box with its thimbleful of cereal out.

In one case, you're being more economical, saving that infinitesimally small bit of toothpaste that would otherwise have been lost forever; in the other, the same volume of cereal gets thrown out, and you are being ever so (albeit negligibly) wasteful — but the greatness of character you've gained in either case is the same. You've been involved in the holy work of perfecting your character. You have gone from being self-centered to other-directed, from being a spoiled, selfish child to a servant of God.

Marriage reaches down deep into the nooks and crannies of your life and your *neshamah*, where tzaddikim are made, and gives you the infinitely precious opportunity to fine-tune your *middot* to a degree undreamed of in earlier, unmarried years.

The greatest goal in any marriage should be to embark on a joint career of aiding and encouraging each other in pursuit of that noblest of all goals: *sheleimut* in *avodat Hashem* — the perfection of one's service of God. Fortunate is the couple who aspires to this lofty, synergistic height. No one beside your spouse could, to the same degree, play this delicate role.

The author of *Cheshbon Hanefesh* writes eloquently and passionately about the importance of having a *chavruta*, a partner, in your quest for spiritual growth and accomplishment. Alone, a person is easily dispirited and discouraged from pursuing the distant goal he has set himself. This is where a *chavruta* plays an all-important role by providing encouragement, advice, and the consoling knowledge that you're not alone, someone is going through this with you. This last piece of information, perhaps more than any other, can spur you on when you would otherwise have given up, disillusioned and frustrated. The Cheshbon Hanefesh concludes this subject with the provocative addendum, "...how much better if that *chavruta* is your wife...."[5]

Marriage, understood for what it is and used properly, is the vehicle, not only for great growth, but also for the most pronounced happiness and fulfillment.

The excellence of character and other spiritual benefits acquired through this process should be recompense enough for all your efforts, but the *Ribono shel Olam* did even more for us: He designed the system such that the more you give and the more you do...the more you get and the more you benefit — in priceless commodities such as happiness and peace of mind.

Of course, as important as it is to know what marriage is, it is equally important to know what marriage is not.

---

5. No. 44.

It is not a panacea.

Marriage is not some magical cure-all. Don't think, because you have found your "perfect" mate, that all your problems will disappear, that somehow — automatically, mystically — your spouse will "save" you or make you whole and complete. Only *you* can do that for yourself. No one else can do it for you. Your spouse is only a prop, a tool, in this regard, albeit a wonderful one — and, as with any tool, is only effective if used correctly.

Also, marriage is not a submersion of the self.

At your wedding, the two of you become a new unity, a new entity (*"ishto kegufo"*)[6] — but that only goes so far. You remain, nevertheless, two distinct individuals with your own identities and obligations to the Almighty. On the Day of Judgment, you won't stand together before Hashem — you'll stand alone.

The philosophy and success of the program described in this book rests on a foundation of six points:

1. Accept the basic, unchangeable facts of your life.

The Almighty knows what He is doing.

Don't say, "I could have succeeded in serving Hashem and in being happy if I had been given a different wife, mother-in-law, etc." Such a belief runs counter to the conviction that Hashem is running the show, that He knows what He is doing. *This* is the situation He "tailor-made" for you. *This* is your opportunity to succeed, your

---

6. *Sanhedrin* 28b.

chance for greatness. *This* and nothing else is exactly what you need.

> *"Kol d'ahvid Rachmana letav ahvid"* — Everything Hashem does is for the good (Berachot 60b).

Don't think it can't be done: "I ended up with a dud — my mazel — and there's nothing I can do about it. If I were married to someone exciting, I could improve my marriage. But what can I do? He/she is a shlemazel."

Not true. Your situation in life is just what the Doctor ordered for you.

2. Commit yourself to the work ahead.

Don't fool yourself. There are no shortcuts or "quick fixes" that will ensure permanent marital success and happiness.

Good marriages don't "just happen"; you have to make them happen. And that requires resolve and hard work. This is not a task undertaken casually or one discharged quickly and easily.

Don't shy away from the task, though. You will be amply rewarded for *any* effort you make. You're going to be married for a lifetime anyway, *iy"H*, so why not invest whatever effort is required to make it an enjoyable, beneficial experience, rather than a mediocre, endurable nuisance? A lifetime of marital happiness and camaraderie — isn't that worth some time and energy?

Are you undaunted by the prospect of some hard

work, drawn by the prize that beckons? Good. Roll up your sleeves (so to speak) and get ready for some good old-fashioned hard work.

3. Improving your marriage begins with improving yourself.

A marriage is made up of two individuals. There is nothing mystical about it. You can't have a good marriage if both partners are selfish, rotten people. Any marriage is only as good as the two people who comprise it. You can't improve your marriage without improving yourself.

The two processes are really one. You start by perfecting yourself — and the perfection of your marriage will quickly and inevitably follow on its heels. Throughout this program, heavy emphasis is placed on techniques for improving you, the individual...who just happens to be one-half of the marriage corporation.

4. It's all in your hands.

Even though you represent only 50% of the partners in your marriage, you can singlehandedly improve your marriage 100% — or more.

Will your spouse want to help you in your campaign to improve your marriage? If you think the answer is yes, then gently inform him that you are about to begin a program designed to make your marriage even better, and invite him to join you.

Does he accept? If so, great. Get two copies and get busy growing together, encouraging and helping each other along. You will complement each other and make giant strides that much more quickly.

Did he decline? No matter. If he is not inclined to join you in the beginning, don't despair. Sure, it would be nice to have his cooperation and participation, but you can still accomplish the worthy goal that you have set for yourself. It may take a little bit longer (not much), but you have all the time in the world, and nothing should derail you. Your unwavering commitment to the success of this project is absolute and unconditional. You're not going to fold at the first sign (or first 100 signs) of setback or failure. Rest assured — before too long, he will join in, *iy"H*. Success and happiness are contagious, and everyone wants to cash in on a good thing.

Remember, though: whether or not your spouse signs on will not affect your behavior towards him one way or the other. You are doing what you do because that is *your* obligation to the Almighty, and to yourself, not because you expect or demand reciprocal treatment.

5. Create your own reality.

Now, the truth is you *always* create your own reality, but you can also *actively* create it, rather than doing what most of us do: passively create it by accepting and operating within the reality someone else (everyone else) foists upon you.

The principle that you create your own reality has some important practical corollaries that are pivotal to the success of this program:

a. There is *always* something meaningful and significant *you can do* to elicit a more positive response from your spouse.

b. Before criticizing others, first look inward. Ask yourself, "What am I doing that is eliciting this undesirable behavior?" Make the necessary corrections and adjustments inside yourself — often, the faults in others will disappear entirely.

c. Act — don't react.

For example, you are nice to your spouse, even a recalcitrant or uncooperative one, *not* because she deserves it (she might not), but, rather, because that is what *you* are supposed to do, that is how Hashem commanded *you* to behave.

Break the linkage between how your spouse behaves towards you and how you respond to your spouse. You no longer "react" to negative stimuli. From now on, you only act. Your actions toward your spouse are completely and solely a function of your fervent desire to improve your marriage, and this desire is completely under your control. The way you responded to your spouse once upon a time may have mirrored the way your spouse behaved towards you — but no more, and never again. That is the best recipe for failure, as minor disturbances are fed back and magnified cyclically a millionfold. Put an end to this silly, destructive feedback cycle. From now on, the spotlight rests squarely where it always belonged — on you, and you alone.

The Baal Shem Tov expressed this truth (that you create your own reality) through a witty reading of a mishnah in *Pirkei Avot* (2:1): "*Da mah lemalah mimcha.*" This is usually translated as, "Know what is above you" (i.e., God). The Baal Shem Tov, however, rendered the mishnah differently: "*Da: mah lemalah* [is] *mimcha*" — know that what is from above (i.e., the reality that the Almighty structures for you) is *from you.*

Our Sages emphasize that this truth is especially appropriate in the institution of marriage. One phrase used by the Torah to describe a wife is *eizer kenegdo*: a helper against him. The Sages explain, "*Zachah* — *eizer;* lo zachah — *kenegdo.*" If the husband is worthy, she is his *eizer*, his helper; if he is not worthy, she is *kenegdo*, she opposes and clashes with him.[7]

The point is, *your* conduct determines and shapes the reality and situation that confronts you.

6. Become an actor.

In *avodat Hashem*, of which marriage is a *big* part, there is no mitzvah to be natural — only successful. The Master of the Universe does not want you to "let it all hang out."

---

7. *Yevamot* 63a.

For the purposes of improving your marriage, you are going to become an actor. You will be called upon often to transcend yourself, to step outside yourself and your instincts for a while. By the time you are done, you will have become convinced that the stage lost a great thespian when you decided instead to pursue a career of service to the Almighty.

Don't feel guilty or hypocritical about acting.

Happily, before too long, you will internalize many of these once orchestrated attitudes and behaviors, and they will become part of your natural repertoire of instincts and emotions.

2

GETTING AN ATTITUDE

Developing Self-Respect and a Healthy Self-Image

HAVING A GOOD, healthy image of yourself is a prerequisite to being able to entertain worthy thoughts of other people — including your spouse.

It is an immutable law of human nature: When a person feels secure and positive about himself, he is much more capable of turning a benevolent eye on the rest of the world.

Conversely, if that person feels empty or angry inside, then the world is a much darker, inhospitable place. Two options confront such a person:

1. struggle up from the imagined abyss in which he

finds himself, or

2. bring everybody else down there with him.

Guess which route most people take. The second option is by far the quicker and easier, albeit the less sound and mentally healthy of the two. Our hapless, unhappy friend turns a grudging, baleful eye on the world and all it has to offer: he "sees" the worst where a more confident person would (correctly) see the best.

Pirkei Avot (1:6) states: "*Asei lecha rav, u'kenei lecha chaver, ve'hevei dan et kol ha'adam lekaf zechut.*" This mishnah is usually translated as, "Make a teacher for yourself, acquire a friend for yourself, and judge every person favorably."

The Ketonet Passim, however, interprets this mishnah differently. According to him, the mishnah presents a sequence of steps, a progression, towards mental health and benevolence.

"*Asei lecha rav*" (make a teacher for yourself) is alternatively translated as "consider yourself important" (rav means "great"). Also, "*kenei lecha chaver*" — acquire and maintain friendships. If you can do these two things — avoid the double dangers of self-deprecation (consider yourself important) and arrogance (the avoidance of which leads to the ability to acquire friends) — only then,[8] the mishnah concludes, "*hevei dan et kol ha'adam lekaf zechut*": because you view yourself positively, you will be able to judge all other people favorably.

---

8. The Ketonet Passim interpolates here the word "*ve'az*" (only then).

Your self-image not only affects how you view others but has dramatic repercussions in how your spouse (and everyone else) views you. Have a high opinion of yourself (without being arrogant or obnoxious), and your spouse will think likewise of you; think poorly of yourself, and, despite her best efforts, in short order your spouse will do the same. The people around you take their cue from you.

> Chana always "downed" herself and her abilities. When she made a cake, she predicted that it would taste lousy. When she bought a dress, she "knew" it wouldn't look good on her. She felt hurt when her husband and children were so critical and unappreciative.
>
> "Why can't you make the kind of cake Mrs. Goldberg makes?"
>
> "The dress would look better if you lost some weight."
>
> However, they were simply echoing her own sentiments.

This fundamental principle — that others tend to view us in the same way we view ourselves — is illustrated by the tragic episode involving the spies whom Moshe Rabbeinu sent to reconnoiter the Land of Israel. The spies conclude their report with the observation, "We were in our own sight as grasshoppers, and so we were in their sight [the natives of Eretz

Yisrael]."[9] The import of their words is pellucid: because the spies, though they were men of great stature and accomplishment in reality, viewed themselves as small and insignificant, the inhabitants of the Land did likewise and adopted the same poor opinion of them.

In sum:

1. Your image of yourself influences your image of the world around you, of which your spouse is a large part.

2. Your image of yourself forms the basis for your spouse's image of you.

Clearly, these phenomena do not occur independently; rather, they are intimately related. One reinforces the other. You'd like to think highly of your spouse, and you'd like your spouse to think highly of you. Both of these depend on *you*, and whether you possess a healthy amount of self-respect.

Following are a few simple rules for acquiring some necessary self-respect.

1. Never speak disparagingly about yourself.

"I look like a horse."

"Sometimes I wonder what you ever saw in me."

"I'm such an idiot!"

"I can't do anything right."

---

9. Bemidbar 13:33.

"I always say the wrong thing."

This is probably the single most important rule to observe in your campaign to improve your marriage.

> *"Machshevet hanefesh nimshach achar hadibbur"* — The thoughts of a person's soul [his fundamental attitudes] are drawn after [influenced by] the words he speaks (Chovot Halevavot).

Words of hope, confidence, and happiness contribute incrementally over the course of years to the creation of a satisfied, optimistic outlook and perspective. Conversely, words of despair, complaint, and dissatisfaction, even flippantly spoken, contribute to the creation of an unhappy, pessimistic personality.

Of course, the effect, for good or bad, of any one comment gets quickly diluted in the jumble of so many other competing, conflicting, thoughtlessly dropped comments. The salutary influence of a positive, happy statement is quickly countered and negated by the equal and opposite deleterious influence of a negative, unhappy one.

If you can confine your comments to the upbeat variety and squelch the negative remarks, in reasonably short order you will begin to notice the astounding consequences of this cardinal principle.

(Convince yourself of the truth and power of the Chovot Halevavot's statement. Try this simple exercise:

Exclaim, "What a beautiful day it is!" *every day* for one month when you survey the out-of-doors for the first time in the morning. You will have the incontrovertible proof you desire.)

Now, if you speak badly about yourself, whatever your original motivation for doing so, then you'll soon start believing your own bad press about yourself. Your self-respect will be severely harmed, with the concomitant result that it will be hard for you to entertain genuine feelings of respect for your spouse or anyone else. In addition, you will convince everybody else that you are not worthy of respect, and they will treat you accordingly. Once you are on this treadmill, it is very hard to get off. The world's disrespectful and disdainful treatment of you (that *you* are responsible for!) will reinforce your already low self-image, causing it to plunge even lower. This is obviously not a good atmosphere in which to try to create a happy marriage. The best way to avoid this problem entirely is not to develop a poor self-image in the first place, and that's where our first rule comes in.

Our Sages caution emphatically against speaking badly about yourself to your spouse (relating, upon your return home from work, yeshivah, or shul the embarrassments and indignities that you suffered that day, for example), and they warn of dire consequences of continuing this foolish practice.[10]

This is probably the most insidious and destructive danger in a marriage, even though most of us remain

---

10. *Avot De R. Natan, beraita,* end of ch. 7; Bartenura, *Avot* 1:5.

unaware of it or dismiss it as insignificant and inconsequential. It seems small and unimportant. It's not. The
cumulative effects of a career of self-deprecating comments are enormous.

At first, the bad image you are working so hard to
create and convince him of cannot compete with the
good, even wonderful, image of you that your spouse
has, the image that motivated him to marry you. Your
spouse will dutifully, sincerely, even vehemently, disagree with you; he will assure you of how wonderful,
smart, competent, clever, and talented you really are and
will scold you for speaking so unflatteringly about yourself.

You'll feel reassured and comforted, but you shouldn't.
Now you should be worried and regretful, because
you've done something terrible. Each self-disparaging
remark leaves a faint impression somewhere in the deep
recesses of his heart, below the level of conscious thought
or awareness. Your spouse's fundamental attitudes towards you have been subtly corrupted. He may never be
aware of it, but you should know that with your comments you have wrought a change in the way your
spouse regards you. You have initiated a process which,
left unchecked, will *"goreim ra'ah le'atzmo"* — cause
you much suffering."[11]

(Perhaps you made that little remark at your own
expense because you were fishing for exactly what you
got — your spouse's reassurance of your considerable

---

11. *Pirkei Avot* 1:5.

worth. That is an unfair and ultimately unwise burden to place on your spouse's shoulders — i.e., to serve as a source of strength for you while absorbing the brunt of all your self-doubt.)

Don't force your spouse to revise his original high opinion of you downwards, even after a lifetime of marriage.

Incorrect

"My boss thinks I'm stupid. I don't think I'll ever figure out how to do this job."

"That's not true. You told me last week that he was very pleased with that report you wrote."

"Yeah, but that was just a stupid, old summary of work someone else did. I can't produce anything new myself."

Correct

"I had a tough day at work. I feel like my boss wants something more from me than what I'm giving."

"Maybe you should speak to one of your coworkers and see if there is something you can do."

"That's a good idea. I know I can do the job. I just need a little more time and guidance."

Incorrect

> "I'm so fat I look like a horse."
>
> "No you don't. You look great."
>
> "What are you talking about? I weigh twenty pounds more than when I got pregnant."
>
> "Well, it doesn't show."
>
> "I couldn't fit into a single outfit in the store!"

Correct

> "I'm trying a new diet."
>
> "Good luck! I'm sure you'll be successful."
>
> "Thanks. I really want to be able to fit into a dress I saw today."

2. Keep a little corner of your world for yourself.

No doubt, before you were married, you did many things that fascinated you and made you a more interesting person. These activities increased your self-esteem as well as your prestige in your *chasan* or *kallah*'s eyes.

Don't drop them all the day you get married.

If you took violin lessons for seventeen years before you were married, don't stop playing the violin the day you get married.

It's true, marriage, children, the responsibility of earning a livelihood, learning, and the ever-increasing complexity of your life put greater demands on the already inadequate amount of time available to you, but find some way to keep up some — even one — of the activities that made you the attractive package your spouse married. And if you did not have one before, or you have outgrown the old ones, get a new one. Give yourself (and your spouse) plenty of cause always to think of you as fascinating, new, ever-fresh, never stale or stagnant.

3. Maintain your physical appearance.

Don't stop exercising or taking care of yourself just because someone was kind enough to marry you. Dress nicely, as you did before you were married, and never walk around the house disheveled and unkempt. And if you insist on looking sloppy in the house, don't compound the offense by getting dressed up nicely afterwards to go to the store.

Don't eat foods that cause bad breath, belching, or worse.

Incorrect

Menachem wore a fashionable suit all day at the office. When he came home from work, he spent the evening lounging around in sweatpants with holes in them. On his day off, he often forgot to shave or comb his hair.

Chana rarely got out of her pajamas in the morning after the birth of her twins. When her husband came home at night, she was disheveled and exhausted. But when her friend invited her out for a ladies' *shiur*, she got dressed up in high heels and makeup.

Correct

A story is told of a pious woman who spent the whole day in her home. While she took care of the house, she wore a beautiful dress. Her makeup was impeccable and she looked elegant. When it was time to go out shopping, she changed into simple clothes and replaced her *sheitel* with a *tichel*. When questioned about this practice, she explained, "My husband is at home. When I'm there, I make myself beautiful for him. Outside the house are other men. For them I don't need to look special."

4. Don't talk too much.

Don't just talk to fill the silence, or to hear yourself talk. You should never speak unless you have something to say.

When you talk, let it be an event of great import. When you open your mouth to speak, your spouse should have ample reason from past experience to believe that something worth listening to is going to come out.

If it is not necessary to talk, it is necessary not to talk.

"Speech is the essential definition of the human soul. So, then, every word that leaves your mouth should be looked upon as an expression of your soul" (R. Chaim of Volozhin).

"What is a person's profession in this world? Let him make himself like a mute" (*Chullin* 89a).

Developing Respect, Gratitude, and Love for Your Spouse

"Hachitzoniyut me'oreret hapenimiyut" — The outside awakens the inside (*Mesilat Yesharim*, end of ch. 7).

One of the most important ingredients in a healthy relationship is respect for each other. However, it is not so simple to generate feelings of respect for a person you have seen in his most vulnerable and unguarded hour. It is much more usual to concentrate on your spouse's weak points than to focus on his more admirable qualities.

We naturally express and display outwardly the emotions and enthusiasms that we feel within. In happier times, your loving behavior and demeanor flow easily and spontaneously from the great love and devotion you feel for your spouse. However, as time goes on, sometimes these feelings wane in the face of family stresses and vicissitudes.

The Mesilat Yesharim teaches us an astounding lesson: "The outside awakens the inside." Your outer behavior can produce powerful *genuine* changes in the fundamental attitudes and emotions buried deep inside you. While your inner feelings may not be open and accessible to direct tinkering, your outer actions definitely *are* susceptible to manipulation and adjustment.

This truth can help you in your efforts to fan the flames of a love that may have cooled. There is no great mitzvah (or advantage) in being natural. Rather, become an actor, and recreate one of the greatest roles you have ever starred in — that of a loving, adoring, excited, enthusiastic husband or wife. The behavior may not come quite so readily and instinctively as it used to, the "lines" that sounded so silky and smooth once upon a time may now more resemble polyester, and you may feel decidedly foolish. Don't. Steel yourself with the knowledge that you are doing the greatest, and smartest, thing you could do: you are creating your own reality, you are perfecting your *middot,* you are reinforcing the integrity of your marriage, you are ensuring for yourself a lifetime of happiness and contentment, and you are being a worthy servant of the Almighty.

Note that you are *not* doing this to fool your spouse into thinking you love him or her; rather you're trying to fool *yourself.* Don't worry: before too long, you'll really believe it.

The following rules will help you stage an "outside" (a repertoire of orchestrated behaviors) that will awaken your "inside" (the reservoir of respect and love for your spouse that you possess).

1. Don't compare your spouse to anyone else.

One of the fundamental building blocks of developing respect is to view your spouse as a unique human being and not judge him against the standards of other people. Appreciate your spouse's special qualities. Focus on what he is doing right as opposed to areas of weakness.

Many women, for example, choose selflessly to build a home and raise a family. These heroic women have passed up the tawdry trappings and glitter of having a career, with the attendant recognition, status, money, and all the myriad benefits that are notably — and sadly — absent in a career of homemaking. Guess where such a woman is most vulnerable. You can destroy your homemaker wife in a moment of anger or thoughtlessness by wondering aloud, "Why are our children the worst behaved children in school?" "Why isn't our house ever neat?" "Why do you drag yourself around like a shlump, unlike so-and-so's wife?" (This last stings worst of all. So-and-so's wife forsook home and children years earlier for the allure of a glamorous career outside the home. It should also be noted that, across town, so-and-so is assailing *his* wife in *her* areas of weakness, and drawing unfavorable comparisons between his wife...and yours.)

Often, the comparisons are not so blatant:

"Why can't you get a job? We need the money. What do you do all day?"

"Leah was back in shul this Shabbat, not even six weeks after her baby was born. Can you believe that?" (You, eight weeks after your baby was born, have still not returned to shul on Shabbat. The implication is clear.)

2. Never speak disparagingly about your spouse in public.

Most of us would adamantly deny (perhaps even resent) the insinuation that we ever violate this rule. We know intuitively that this is a very low thing to do, and we would never sink to the level of being so disloyal and despicable.

We're forgetting the "just joking" syndrome.

Don't say unkind things at your spouse's expense, even if you immediately excuse them afterwards with the explanation that you were "just joking."

The harm to be had from violating this rule is not just the slight to your spouse's honor (although that is itself no small thing). The other great danger lies in the fact that, by opening your mouth, you can talk yourself into a lot of dumb attitudes and ideas. You think you are being witty or socially clever? Maybe, but you're also being disloyal and cruel to your spouse, and destructive to yourself.

For example, don't insult the holy institution of marriage. Many people, upon hearing news of a friend's engagement, "congratulate" their friend this way: "Well, old buddy, you're making the same mistake we all made...."

Aside from being disloyal to your spouse, you have talked yourself, ever so slightly, into believing something that you didn't really believe before. And, on top of that, you have "infected" your friend with the "disease" of discontent and unhappiness. Why did you do all these terrible things? For the sake of a joke?

> Levity destroys a person's heart such that reason and knowledge no longer rule over him.... With one bit of levity a person can deflect from himself a multitude of influences and stimuli that would encourage him to examine his ways.... The force of levity is such that it destroys many facets of ethical thinking and fear of God....
>
> (*Mesilat Yesharim*)

For the same effort, you can say something like: "That's terrific. Marriage is a wonderful thing, and you got a great girl. *Baruch Hashem*, you are very lucky...."

You'll bolster your friend's morale, and, at the same time, you'll be promoting your own psychological and emotional well-being.

And, if you want to be a tzaddik, say something like: "I hope your wife will give you as much happiness as my extraordinary wife gives me, *iy"H*."

A group of young couples were trading humorous anecdotes about being newly-weds. Devora joked about Dovid's first encounter with a washing machine. Then she related how it takes him 2½ hours to do the shopping. The couples laughed up-roariously. Dovid smiled good-naturedly, but felt slightly betrayed; he did not especially enjoy being the butt of everybody's humor.

Instead of mocking her husband, Devora should have complimented her husband's attempts to be helpful and talked about the many successes he'd already had.

3. Don't give your spouse insulting nicknames.

Even if your intentions are entirely loving, don't allow an unkind or unflattering word to cross your lips.

Don't call your spouse "cutesie" or insulting nick-names like "spacey" or "yentie."

Try "Darling," "Beautiful," "Handsome," or "Honey" instead.

4. Always say "please" and "thank you."

Among the character traits we are expected to de-velop, a very prominent one is the ability to feel and express gratitude to the Almighty for the infinite number of blessings that He bestows upon us.

But it is hard to grasp even a small amount of His benevolence towards us. It is far — infinitely far —

removed from our sphere of experience. We are not accustomed to such a mode of behavior — i.e., to give selflessly, tirelessly, unstintingly, in every facet of the human experience. And yet, that is what the Almighty does for each of us. How can we relate meaningfully to Hashem's infinite benevolence? How can our minds grasp and contain this truth?

The Creator recognized our dilemma and supplied a solution. To provide us with a meaningful analogy, from which we can extrapolate and try, in our limited way, to comprehend the *Ribono shel Olam*'s benevolence better, He gives us husbands and wives. They serve as a model of such multifaceted benevolence, showering us with the blessings of food, children, clothing, home, love, security, comfort, etc. There is an intimate connection between the ability to feel gratitude to your spouse and the capacity to recognize and appreciate the kindnesses bestowed by the Almighty. The first step, then, in learning how to "adequately" express gratitude to Him is learning how to express our appreciation to His emissary.

Our Sages teach, "All who deny the good done for them by people will ultimately deny the good done for them by Hashem Himself."[12] Significantly, the Sages derive this from their observation of the very first marriage between Adam and Chava.

When you ask your spouse to do something for you, introduce your request with the word "please." When

---

12. *Avodah Zarah* 5b.

your spouse does something nice for you, say "thank you." Remind yourself that your spouse is not your servant. This simple exercise in decency will give you valuable training in feeling respect and gratitude toward your spouse.

5. Do one nice thing for your spouse every day.

> "You love him to whom you give, *not* him who gives to you" (R. Eliyahu Dessler, *Kuntres Hachessed*, ch. 5).

We know that a person gives happily and bountifully to someone he loves. This is obvious; we see it every day.

Not only does that loving gesture express your love, R. Dessler points out, but your love is further deepened and enhanced by your loving act. Give again, and more plentifully, and your love is amplified yet again. This wonderful cycle continues on and on.

Don't be deceived, R. Dessler cautions, into thinking that you love the person who gives to you. That love is, at best, shallow and fleeting, and is little more than dressed-up self-love. True love is selfless love, giving love.

If that's the case, there must be some way to exploit the "amplification" effect inherent in the love-give-love-give cycle. There is, *b"H*. Give. Jump right in. Start giving to your spouse. There are no requirements or prerequisites. Give, and you'll feel something stirring deep in your soul. Give again, and that small, still voice will push its way to the fore.

The act of giving doesn't need to be flamboyant,

expensive, or grandiose; it only needs to be frequent and consistent.

Start today. Buy your husband or wife a loving (kosher!) greeting card, write something romantic inside, attach it to a modest gift (all the things that once came so naturally when you were busy courting each other), and give it to him.

Don't do this only once, or it will go unnoticed or be dismissed (by you, that is) as an aberration, and be promptly forgotten (by you) before it can begin to work its magic. Keep it up, and repeat such acts of giving every day.

As part of your daily routine, spend time thinking what nice little gesture you can do for your spouse, where you can take her, what kinds of gifts he would like, etc. Use your imagination. Force yourself to create, if artificially for now, enthusiasm and excitement over the woman or man you married. Don't worry — it'll come more quickly and naturally before too long. Let — even force — thoughts of your spouse to pervade your waking hours. Gently, but forcefully, push any negative thoughts and emotions you may feel towards your spouse to the back of your mind — and then out entirely. You're too busy right now ensuring your everlasting success and happiness to be distracted by extraneous and useless mental or emotional diversions.

6. Say one nice thing to your spouse every day.

Don't stumble through your marriage, oblivious of your spouse. Be aware of your spouse's needs and sensitive to her vulnerabilities. Encourage your spouse, especially in those vulnerable areas. Offer, before you are asked or begged, the reassurance, encouragement, and praise that all of us want and need.

Get into the habit of complimenting your spouse lavishly, extravagantly even. It doesn't cost you anything, so don't be parsimonious in your praise.

These kind words serve double-duty. They make your spouse feel great. In addition, as the Chovot Halevavot teaches us, they will inspire you with positive attitudes towards your spouse.

Here are some ideas:

> "You (your hair, clothes, etc.) look beautiful (handsome)."
>
> "I thought you spoke well (said the right thing)."
>
> "I like the game you made up for Rivka tonight."

3

COMMUNICATING

Learning How to Communicate with Your Spouse

THE SINGLE GREATEST skill in creating and ensuring a good marriage is the ability to communicate well. If you and your spouse can communicate well with each other, you are on your way to a great marriage; if either of you cannot communicate well, learn how — there is no alternative.

It is telling that the very first sin was committed, according to some authorities, because of a lack of communication between the first husband and wife. The Creator forbade *eating* from the Tree of Knowledge, but Adam, in relating the Almighty's prohibition to his wife, forbade her to eat from or *touch* the Tree. He neglected to mention that the prohibition against touching the tree was a safety measure he had enacted to protect Hashem's commandment.

The snake shrewdly capitalized on this failure in communication. He showed Chava that no danger resulted from touching the tree. Therefore, he reasoned, why not eat from it as well? The snake's argument seemed convincing to Chava, since she did not know that Hashem had only forbade eating from the tree, not touching it. Adam failed to properly communicate the distinction between Hashem's directive and his own enactment.

Following are some basic ground rules for learning how to communicate well.

1. Good communication is mostly good listening.

Learn how to listen to your spouse. Sometimes you have to go beyond and behind what you hear, beyond and behind the words your spouse is saying — what is she trying to tell you? The words you are hearing and what your spouse is trying to communicate to you are not always the same.

For example, a rapid-fire string of complaints about a lot of inconsequential things you may have done — things which usually go unnoticed, about which he does not comment or care in normal times — might indicate that your spouse is unhappy for some reason and is venting some anger or frustration, or is sending out a cry for help. The wrong thing to do is get muddled up in those misleading complaints. Identify and help solve that other problem, and the string of complaints will disappear by itself.

Don't invoke this principle universally, however, dismissing every complaint that comes your way as a symptom of some other problem that is distressing your partner. Be honest. With time — and mistakes, it's true — you can learn how to distinguish between real complaints and the "distress signal" variety.

> Shmuel was having trouble at work and was concerned he might lose his job. He returned home disgruntled and irascible. Instead of confiding in his wife and telling her his concerns, he started complaining that the house was a mess and that his dinner wasn't ready.

> Sarah was feeling overwhelmed by the children, work, and all her responsibilities at home. She felt that Shmuel did not help her as much as he could, and, more importantly, that he wasn't very sympathetic to her. Instead of talking about what was really bothering her and asking for more help around the house and with the children, she started complaining about her husband's overindulgent attitude towards his parents, his constant invitations to them for Shabbat and holidays, and all the things her in-laws do and say to annoy her.

2. Learn to talk about things that are bothering you. Don't let tensions build up.

It is dangerous to keep problems bottled up inside. They will "eat away at you," with disastrous results, *ch"v*. Even a relatively small problem, if left unattended, can smoulder, become magnified over time, and assume proportions far beyond what reality would dictate. Express — force yourself, if necessary, to express — hurts and issues as you experience them.

(Of course, it is never wise to discuss an emotional issue in the heat of the moment. Wait until the initial displeasure has subsided and, in a calm moment, resolve the problem as quickly and as coolly as possible.)

But within reason. Don't be a "kvetcher." Don't make a big deal over every little slight — real or imagined — to your precious honor. Know when to "let it go."

3. Set fixed times for communicating.

If either of you does not communicate your feelings easily, naturally, and spontaneously, then consider setting fixed times for talking — weekly or daily "rap sessions," so to speak. How often you schedule your sessions should depend on your individual needs.

These meetings might be informal and free-wheeling, or "structured" — for example, each partner might be required to volunteer "one thing you did today (this week) which I appreciated" in order to lubricate communication, until, *i"yH*, communicating becomes a natural part of your repertoire. The frequency, length, and structure of these sessions can be varied depending on circumstances, personalities, and a variety of other factors.

Learning How to Criticize, Persuade, and Influence Your Spouse

There are times, perhaps, when it is necessary to criticize your spouse (but only *after* you have satisfied yourself that you have done everything you can to ensure that you are not the root cause of the problem).

But criticize wisely.

Most people criticize in such a way that their comments just can't be accepted; no matter how right in substance they might be, their delivery precludes any chance of success. As soon as you put your spouse on the defensive, it's all over; you've lost your chance of getting your point across.

Presumably, if you feel the need to criticize your spouse, it's because you want to convince him to change some behavior or attitude. (About criticizing for the sake of criticizing, without some practical objective of improvement, there is nothing to be said. It is but one of many forms of psychological cruelty.) When you are confronted with a behavior or attitude in your partner that you do not like, your "natural" reaction might be one of anger, scorn, or derision. But, as we have said, *there is no mitzvah to be natural.* These are bad reactions, and you shouldn't give expression to them. On top of that, these reactions are not effective. They won't accomplish anything positive; in fact, they are guaranteed 100% counterproductive.

The following rules will take the "sting" out of your criticism:

1. Don't terrorize, tyrannize, dictate, or demand.

You can't force (physically or psychologically) another person (even your spouse) to behave the way *you* want her to behave.

Accept and respect the fact that your spouse is an autonomous person — and an intelligent one at that.

Incorrect

"I do not want you to speak with Miriam anymore. All you do is say *lashon hara.*"

Correct

"Perhaps you should consider pursuing some other friendships besides your friendship with Miriam. There are some very fine women in the neighborhood whom you would really like."

The following midrash provides us with our next three rules:

Regarding the verse in Tehillim, "Hashem, do not rebuke me in Your anger," R. Elazar said: [To understand David Hamelech's request, i.e., how Hashem rebukes without anger] consider the parable of a king who, while holding a sharp sword in his hand, became angry at his son and, in his rage, swore to strike the sword over his son's head. The king immediately reconsidered, "If I strike him thus, he won't be able to survive the blow, and who will inherit my kingdom? But, to nullify my decree is impossible."

What did the king do?

He slid the sword into its sheath and struck the blunted sword over his son's head, with the result that he did not injure his son, nor did he nullify his decree.

R. Levi said: [To understand how Hashem rebukes without anger] consider the parable of a king who became angry at his son and, in his rage, swore to strike him with one hundred ropes. The king immediately reconsidered, "If I lash him thus, he won't be able to survive, and who will inherit my kingdom? But, to nullify my decree is impossible."

What did the king do?

He took a single rope, folded it over one hundred times into one hundred small rope segments, and struck him once with this small, blunt instrument, with the result that he did not injure his son, nor did he nullify his decree.

R. Huna said: [To understand how Hashem rebukes without anger] consider the parable of a king before whom lay an enormous boulder. The king became angry at his son and, in his rage, swore to hurl the boulder at his son. The king immediately reconsidered, "If I hurl this at him, he won't be able to survive the blow, and who will inherit my kingdom? But, to nullify my decree is impossible."

What did the king do?

He crushed the huge boulder into tiny pebbles and threw each little pebble at his son one at a time, with the result that he did not injure his son, nor did he nullify his decree.

(*Yalkut Tehillim* 6)

What does this midrash mean?

The Peninei Hasheleimut suggests that the Sages, through their parables, are describing three different hazards of giving criticism and are offering three alternative methods for how to criticize without anger.

2. Don't criticize destructively (R. Elazar's sword parable).

When you have a complaint against your

fellow, consider that, perhaps, with your acerbic, acrimonious, *sharp* words and delivery you will only ruin, and not fix at all....

(*Peninei Hasheleimut*)

Rather, a critique should be soft, so as to accomplish the most while inflicting the least pain.

Your reason for criticizing your spouse must be solely altruistic (to encourage his improvement), *not* to prove your superiority or to make him feel inferior or stupid. Subjecting someone to a withering onslaught of insensitive, harsh criticism in order to prove beyond doubt that he is wrong and, more importantly, that you are right is unconscionable. It is, ironically, the best method to guarantee defiance as well as the perpetuation, reinforcement, and intensification of the behavior you are trying to eliminate.

Incorrect

"You never help me with the kids because you're inconsiderate and selfish, just like your father."

Correct

"I know you're tired, but it would really help me a lot if you could get the kids in pajamas."

3. Distinguish between symptoms and causes (R. Levi's rope parable).

In this parable, the one hundred ropes represent different manifestations of a single problem. The one rope folded over many times represents the true underlying problem.

> If you have many complaints against your fellow and you unloose all your criticisms at one time, his soul will loathe and reject you and you will accomplish nothing. Rather than offer many criticisms, isolate, identify, and concentrate only on the source of his improper behavior, and, through correcting the source, all the symptoms will automatically work themselves out and disappear.
>
> *(Peninei Hasheleimut)*

Try not to criticize symptoms. It's a big waste of time. Instead, try to identify and address the underlying causes that motivate the behaviors you find objectionable. Take care of the causes and the symptoms will disappear by themselves.

Incorrect

> "You come home, leave your coat on the chair, leave your dirty dishes on the table, and expect me to wait on you like a maid."

Correct

"I know you're tired at the end of the day. After you relax for a few minutes, could you possibly try to clean up a little? Because I'm tired, too."

4. Don't pile it on (R. Huna's rock parable).

When you have a large, multifarious complaint (or many complaints) against your fellow, consider whether this heavy barrage will injure and damage with the crushing impact of a large boulder and only shock him and cause him to despair.

Instead, crumble your complaint into smaller, easily digested complaints (each one of which can be accepted) and then, every once in a while, inform him of one of them and he will be able to accept it easily.

(*Peninei Hasheleimut*)

If you have five complaints against your spouse, don't voice them all at the same time. Choose the most pressing one and discuss it with your spouse. Then, *in two months, choose the next entry on your list and discuss that one. Don't unveil all your criticisms at the same time.*

Incorrect

"You spend too much money, you're always talking on the phone, the house is a mess, and I'm sick of your sister's kids coming over all the time."

Correct

"We have to figure out some way to cut back on our expenses. Is there anything we can do to save money that you can think of?"

A few months later: "I so enjoy talking with you, but the phone always seems to interrupt our conversations. Why don't we turn off the phone in the evening during supper and have some quiet time together, free of distraction?"

5. Don't nag.

Don't say the same thing over and over and over and over again. It's annoying.

6. Encourage good behaviors through honest compliments.

Don't manipulate through insincere compliments or engage in any other form of psychological treachery.

Compliment sincerely, with genuine admiration.

Compliment specifically, not vaguely.

Compliment enthusiastically, not grudgingly or half-heartedly.

7. Criticize constructively.

If you are going to give criticism, do it in such a way that your spouse can accept it — gently and sparingly. Allow your spouse to retain his dignity and sense of self-worth throughout; in fact *increase* them. Remind your spouse through your manner that you aren't the enemy; you are an ally and a concerned friend. Your only interest is your spouse's well-being and betterment. Offer your criticism; don't bludgeon her over the head with it. Suggest a different perspective for your spouse's consideration; don't demand that your spouse accept it. If your style is not threatening, there is a good chance you'll be listened to.

> *"Devarim hayotzim min haleiv nichnasim el haleiv"* — Words that come from the heart enter the heart (see Alshich, Devarim 6:6).

> *"Divrei chachamim benachat nishmaim"* — Words of the wise, if spoken softly and gently, are accepted and listened to (Kohelet 9:17).

And don't forget the most effective and persuasive technique of all:

8. Influence your spouse through your own steady personal example.

You can accomplish some pretty amazing things

using this wonderful technique — usually *without having to say a single word of criticism*. It may take a little longer, and you may not get the recognition you think you deserve for being right, but its effects are deep, real, and permanent — and isn't that what you are interested in?

Learning How to Fight (Cleanly) with Your Spouse

Let's face it. You're going to have fights.

A wise man once gave me the following *berachah*: "I wish you a wife who fights well." I was perplexed. That's a *berachah*?

That *is* a *berachah*. There *will* be fights — that's natural. There *will* be problems — that's inevitable. Your first fight — or first ten fights — should not send you into a tailspin of doubts and recriminations and convince you that you've made a huge and costly mistake. You haven't. You're going through what everybody else goes through. You're learning how to be married.

You can control and minimize the scope, magnitude, and intensity of any fight that comes your way. Here are some pointers:

1. Never start a fight.

Find some other way to communicate your displeasure.

2. Don't cause a fight.

Don't act in a way that annoys or infuriates your spouse.

3. Don't talk if you don't have to. Say as little as possible.

Anything you say in the "heat" of battle (or out of it, for that matter) can — and will — be used against you. Maybe not immediately, but it *will* be used — and remembered. When you fight, you say things you wouldn't otherwise say when your intellect is exercising discretion, when "cooler" heads prevail. You'll only regret it later. So the less you say, the better.

4. Before responding to any provocation, wait a few seconds.

Force yourself to wait those few precious seconds until that first, fiercest wave of anger and indignation passes.

> "A wise person possesses seven traits: …he does not answer rashly…" (*Pirkei Avot* 5:9).

5. Consider: crazy as it sounds, maybe your spouse is right.

Force yourself to consider this possibility. Maybe your spouse is right, and you are wrong.

Don't do this exercise half-heartedly. Transcend yourself for a moment. Even if you decide ultimately that you are right, your momentary excursion of imagination may give you some insight or show you some merit to the other side of the argument. If you can find some legitimacy in your spouse's contention, you are already on the road to resolution and reconciliation.

And, if you realize that you *are* wrong, admit that you are wrong. Who knows, someday your spouse may return the favor!

> "A wise person possesses seven traits: …he admits the truth..." (*Pirkei Avot* 5:9).

> "We have erred…, recognized our error, and, in spite of this, maintained our position rather than admit the truth" (from the alphabetical confessional of R. Chaim Yosef David Azulai).

6. Check your emotions at the door.

Keep your cool.

"With a little practice, you can learn to emotionally leave a situation" (Zelig Pliskin, *Gateway to Happiness*, p. 313).

This is an excellent skill to acquire!

7. Stick to the subject.

Don't rehash every "crime" your partner has ever committed. Don't wander far afield, dredging up other issues, problems, and complaints. Keep this squabble as localized as possible. Don't globalize — or exaggerate, for that matter.

> "A wise person possesses seven traits: ...he sticks to the subject..." (*Pirkei Avot* 5:9).

8. Don't be jealous for your own honor.

Thrice daily we pray (in the *Elokai Netzor* after *Shemoneh Esrei*): "...let my soul be [humble] like dust to everyone...." Do we ever try to fulfill this — that for which we daven so fervently — even once in our lives? Give it a try the next time you find yourself being assailed.

Let it go. Don't respond.

> "Our Rabbis taught about those who are insulted but do not insult in turn, those who hear themselves being disgraced but do not respond. Regarding such people the verse [Shoftim 5] says, 'Let them that love Him be as the sun when it comes out in its might' " (*Shabbat* 88b, *Yoma* 23a).

> "Fortunate is he who hears himself being shamed but remains silent...because of his silence one hundred evils pass him by..." (Rashi, *Sanhedrin* 7a).

> "Hashem forgives the sins of those who act with forbearance.... If a person acts leniently regarding slights to his own honor,

so, too, Hashem is lenient when judging such a person" (*Rosh Hashanah* 17a and Rashi there).

9. Realize where it's really coming from and who is really responsible for this.

It's coming from you...:

> The Almighty runs the world according to the system of "*middah keneged middah*" — measure for measure. That is, in the manner in which a man behaves towards Hashem, so his wife behaves towards him.... If he rebels against the *Ribono shel Olam*, then [the Almighty works things out such that] his wife rebels against him. Accordingly, any *ben Torah* whose wife does not get along with him should know that the cause of this is his own conduct towards Hashem, and therefore he should not complain about his wife, since he is the one who caused himself his problems.
>
> (R.A. Azulai, *Chessed L'Avraham, Ein Yaakov,* no. 48.)

...through Hashem:

> David Hamelech, with all his righteousness and clinging to Hashem... only merited to become the "fourth wheel of the Divine Chariot" because of his patience and for-

bearance, such as that he exhibited when he restrained himself from getting angry at Shimmi ben Geira after Shimmi threw dirt at him, abused him, cursed him, and hurled stones at him. What was David's reaction [to Shimmi's outrageous provocation]? "Leave him be and let him curse, for it is Hashem who commanded him: Curse!"

(Matok Medevash)

So why should you be angry at your spouse?

10. Don't disrupt the normal routine.

"Don't leave your place…" (Kohelet 10:4).

Don't hop a plane to California. Maintain the normal routine of the family. Attend to your responsibilities both in and out of the house, even though you just don't feel like it. Go to work. Make dinner. Adhering to the usual pattern of life provides a framework for the eventual restoration of normalcy.

11. Don't "go for the jugular."

Remember one basic fact: this is your spouse whom you love, whom you married. You've built — and are building — a life together. If that's the standard against which you are measuring this issue, you won't exaggerate its importance.

Be careful how you define "winning." All's *not* fair in love and war. Don't be cruel. Don't say things that you know will infuriate or enrage your spouse. Don't allow yourself the freedom of saying anything you have to in order to prove your point, to "win this round." You could very possibly win this battle, and, at the same time, lose the whole war. Even in the heat of battle, remember who your "opponent" is.

> *"Berogez racheim tizkor"* — Amid rage, remember to be merciful" (Chavakuk 3:2).

12. Generate feelings of love for your spouse.

> One should say [to himself], "...once there was an earlier time when that other person had not yet acted improperly, and in that earlier time he was a worthy person." Let him remember the good which the other person did in his youth, let him recall the love he received when he was a young child; in this way, there is no person who does not awaken our sympathies and is not worthy of our kindness and mercy....
> *(Tomer Devorah, Middah* 13)

Once that nagging wife was your beautiful young *kallah*; once that opinionated, selfish husband was your handsome new *chasan*. Mentally slip away for a moment from your brawl and take a quick trip down Memory Lane. When you return a moment later, to rejoin that fight already in progress, you may be surprised to find that your anger has subsided and your interest in this fight has waned.

13. Don't name-call.

14. Leave your in-laws out of it.

Don't draw comparisons between your spouse and his parents. Don't say things like, "You're just like your mother/father."

15. Men: Don't say, "You're about to get your period (so you're out of control)."

16. Never fight in front of your children.

Don't use your innocent children as weapons, and don't try to rally them to your side.

A child's sense of security and confidence are a function of the peace within the home and the marital harmony and love between husband and wife. Children are filled with uncertainty and dread when they see their parents fight. Even a few heated words exchanged between husband and wife — not even enough to raise the ire of either partner — can send a child into paroxysms of fear and confusion.

If you must disagree or fight, do it quietly behind closed (sound-proof) doors after the children have gone to sleep.

If you observe these rules and don't lose your head, you'll ensure that every fight is not intensified, is conducted civilly, and is resolved — or at least ended — quickly.

4

MARITAL INTIMACY

A COMPREHENSIVE DISCUSSION of the laws and philosophy of *Taharat Hamishpachah* is beyond the scope of this book and, for our purposes here, unnecessary. There is no shortage of excellent books on the subject, and our discussion in no way treats exhaustively the manifold physical, emotional, psychological, and spiritual blessings that are to be had from a career of faithful observance of *taharat hamishpachah*.

Instead, we will confine our discussion to a few comments and observations about the *niddah* discipline and some of its unexpected dividends, and we will endeavor to point out how the *niddah* discipline serves as a vehicle for expressing many lessons presented in this book.

Without a doubt, in no other sphere of the human

experience have we so totally assimilated the attitudes of the non-Jewish world than in our attitudes towards marital intimacy. This is particularly sad, since in this realm they have little of value to say to us.

Even as decadent 20th-century society wallows in unbridled sensuality, it continues to transmit the subliminal message that such things are inherently evil and incompatible with nobler concepts of morality, decency, and religion (a great falsehood taught to the world by Christianity). "It's 'bad,' but it's fun, so we're going to revel in it" — that's the guilt-inspiring message of the value makers in the media (e.g., film, music, fashion, press), exemplified by the song writer who wails, "I'd rather laugh with the sinners than cry with the saints. The sinners are much more fun." Those who fashion public values refuse to allow it to emerge into the daylight of morality under the unblinking sun of religious values and sensibilities, preferring, instead, to hold it hostage in their netherworld of the secular and profane.

In Judaism, marital intimacy is *not* inherently bad or evil. But, like everything else, it *is* subject to abuse — as secular society has convincingly demonstrated. Judaism, using *taharat hamishpachah* as a vehicle, hallows marital relationships. In a typically psychologically healthy fashion, Judaism encourages loving marital intimacy while demanding moderation and self-control.

Before my marriage, the following piece of "conventional wisdom" was offered to me by my non-Jewish coworkers: Set aside a jar. Every time you and your spouse have marital intimacy during the first three years of marriage, deposit a penny; after that, every time the two of you have intimacy, subtract a nickel (that is, remove five pennies). "You'll never empty the jar!" concluded my well-meaning, albeit misguided, coworkers triumphantly.

Why they felt so triumphant I never figured out. The sense of despair and defeat contained in this dark vision of the inevitable deterioration of marriage was overwhelming. Thank God, the principles of a Jewish marriage differ fundamentally from the "typical" ill-fated, doomed marriage they depicted.

How does *taharat hamishpachah* make intimacy into the noble and esteemed pursuit that Judaism considers it, as opposed to the depraved activity of the non-Jewish world? Simply by protecting the couple from the destructive overindulgence that characterizes relationships which have no outer restraints.

There is more to the marital relationship than the physical act for its own sake. There is the "psychic" component of the relationship — the psychological, emotional, and spiritual factors — that goes hand-in-hand with the physical component; these are inextricably bound up. If the psychic component is missing, the physical cannot long provide the real, substantive satisfaction and fulfillment that people need from intimacy. In the above example of overindulgence in the first three years of marriage, the psychic element is notably absent, with the inevitable result that marital intimacy soon inspires feelings of disappointment, emptiness, and betrayal.

Built into the *niddah* discipline is the appreciation of the crucial role of the psychic component in marital intimacy. Each precious element is given its due attention.

The Torah literature speaks of the honeymoon that is revisited and recreated every month for the couple who observes *taharat hamishpachah* properly. That is an ambitious goal. How does the *niddah* discipline purport to accomplish this?

The first intimate encounter is characterized by more than just physical enjoyment; there is much more to distinguish it from subsequent encounters. There is the excitement, the novelty and freshness, the anticipation —the all-important psychic ingredients. While the physical elements of that first encounter are easily duplicated, the psychic rarely, if ever, are duplicated, or even approximated. *This* is the gift of *taharat hamishpachah*, to recreate the conditions under which the psychic element of the marriage bond can flourish.

Full marital success, fulfillment, and happiness is impossible without the meticulous observance of the *niddah* laws. The marriage relationship cannot flower to its fullest potential for mutual trust and respect without observance of *taharat hamishpachah*. Nevertheless, its observance is *not* a foolproof guarantee of these benefits. Adherence to the intricate laws of *niddah* is a *necessary*, but not *sufficient*, condition to ensure the full actualization of the blessings that marriage has to offer. As the Ramban ruefully observes in his commentary on the Torah's command of "*kedoshim tihiyu,*"[13] there is always some way to "beat the system" if you've got your heart set — foolishly — on doing so.

The Torah lifestyle is the stated will of the Almighty — and the most perfect, satisfying lifestyle possible, *if* you allow *it* to guide *you.* It is possible to live a lifetime in technical observance of the laws of *niddah,* all the while spectacularly failing to learn some of its more subtle, delicate lessons. You can punctiliously discharge all halachic obligations but stubbornly refuse to allow its spirit to pervade you, to animate you.

In order to accomplish its ambitious goals, *taharat hamishpachah* must be viewed and approached as a means of attaining marital bliss — *not* as one more difficult limitation in a life filled with restrictions.

The halachic requirements of *taharat hamishpachah* are specific and clear. Many of the following rules reiterate halachic requirements. They are listed here in order to emphasize their importance on an emotional level. In order to optimize the psychological benefits of observing *taharat hamishpachah,* these halachot and the spirit that pervades them must be carefully observed.

1. Hands off!

Among those who have kept the *niddah* laws for

---

13. Vayikra 19:2.

years, there are some who still allow themselves casual hugs or pecks on the cheek during the separation period. In order to enjoy the full benefits of *niddah*, the physical separation between husband and wife during the *niddah* period must be scrupulously observed and *absolute*, without interruption or exception.

Does this seem unnecessarily harsh, or oppressive? It's not. No aspect of this perfect lifestyle is the product of arbitrary whim or caprice. Every ingredient plays its unique role in creating an atmosphere of mental health, peace of mind, tranquility, and contentment, free of guilt or shame. Moreover, there is nothing to compare to the jubilation of reuniting with a loved one after a *true* separation of twelve days.

2. Respect your spouse's privacy.

Marital intimacy is a privilege of marriage, not a right. The *niddah* laws don't allow you to forget that or to take marital intimacy for granted.

Each spouse is an individual, with a right to his or her privacy. *Niddah* respects and protects that right.

How?

In a marriage not governed by Torah values, no real privacy exists. An overture that is not reciprocated may result in feelings of hurt, disappointment, or suspicion that the declining partner is no longer interested or satisfied by the relationship. There can be no period for recuperation free of the looming specter of hurt and rejection.

In contrast, in a marriage shaped by the laws of *taharat hamishpachah*, a separation is mandated by halachah. The Torah creates, thereby, an externally imposed atmosphere of privacy in the relationship. Each partner knows that a violation of his or her partner's privacy during this part of the month is expressly forbidden.

In this way *niddah* creates a safe haven in time into which each partner can withdraw to regroup and recoup the delicate mental and emotional energies that can be exhausted during sustained periods of physical intimacy.

3. Don't waste the "off time" of the month.

The days of separation provide a unique opportunity for interacting in a non-physical way, to be *"re'im ahuvim,"* confidants and loving friends. Communication of the non-physical variety is the only means of interaction available to you. It is a time to be cherished and carefully guarded. Don't consider that part of the month a "goner" or "lost cause" and schedule all your late night meetings (work, yeshivah school board, etc.) for those days. This will simply frustrate this God-given opportunity for meaningful interaction as two equal, intelligent, and loving partners who possess respect and admiration for one another.

During the "off time" of the month, work on the emotional component of the bonds that unite you and your spouse. Talk to each other. Go for a walk together. Have something to do with each other. Spend some time alone together — calm, relaxed, friendly time together.

Take care, though, not to violate the prohibition

against physical contact during your time together. Relapsing into the physical modes of expressing affection is tempting, but is strictly forbidden by the Torah and will only frustrate your ultimate goals.

The *niddah* period provides an opportunity to build a relationship through words rather than actions. This ability to communicate verbally (and not with a kiss or a hug) is sometimes a neglected and forgotten art with couples who have been together for a while. The skills you acquire and hone during the *niddah* period remain long after that period has ended, and they supplement and enhance the physical modes of expression during the "on time" of the month when marital intimacy is allowed and encouraged.

If the cessation of marital intimacy is meticulously observed and the days of separation are used how they were intended — namely, for the reawakening, reaffirming, strengthening, and deepening of the emotional bond between husband and wife — then the significance and enjoyment of the physical component of the marriage relationship, when it is resumed some days later, will be deepened and intensified immeasurably. Wedded to the emotional bond that unites husband and wife, the physical relationship between them takes on wholly new dimensions, importance, and enjoyment. No longer some necessary compromise or submission to the "animal" or base aspect of humanity, marital intimacy is instead seen for what it really is — or what it was intended to be: a noble vehicle for the expression of love and affection for your spouse.[14]

Do not view the *niddah* period as a wasted or deprived time. Instead, recognize and exploit the unique opportunity it provides you for deepening and enhancing your relationship.

4. Develop problem-solving techniques during the *niddah* period.

Too often, when confronted with a problem, people opt to take the "easy way out" and "solve" their problems physically — i.e., in the bedroom. Not only does this not work, but it exacerbates the original problem and even introduces a few new ones of its own.

The delicate, crucial role of intimacy in a marriage is thereby cheapened and degraded; it assumes an unnatural role — that of a substitute for honest talk and open, substantive dialogue. Each partner loses respect for the other, viewing him as ultimately shallow and unworthy if he can so effortlessly, easily, and willingly be placated and distracted. And, on top of it all, the original problem remains somewhere in abeyance, festering. Rest assured, it will return "when you least expect it," and this time it will be much more ferocious. You will either be forced to "cop out" again by resorting to a physical "solution," or this time you will have to face it deprived of your most powerful and effective weapons — the ability to communicate with each other and regard

---

14. See R. Hirsch on *Vayikra* 18:6.

each other with respect.

When disagreements occur during the *niddah* period, a physical encounter is not an option. A couple is forced to discuss, compromise, apologize, and get back on even ground without the crutches of physical contact. Clear communication and loving and gentle words are the only recourse at this time of the month.

5. Satisfy your partner.

Intimacy is one of the means available to express your tender feelings for your spouse. A word of caution: A woman's physical satisfaction is intimately tied up with her emotional satisfaction. A man can enjoy intimacy even when things are not *perfect* emotionally. A woman cannot. When a woman's emotional needs are not being met, she might begin to feel used and start to nurse some dangerous notions such as, "my husband doesn't care about *me*, only about my body." Spending quality time together is an important prelude to intimacy. Don't neglect this aspect of satisfying each other.

The learning process young couples go through can be fraught with uncertainty and bewilderment. Don't be afraid to discuss (discreetly and respectfully) marital intimacy with your spouse. Communicate your needs, fears, etc., to your spouse modestly, but without shame. A couple can acquire an enormous amount of trust through this shared learning process.

5

PROBLEM AREAS

Parents and In-laws

IT MUST BE STATED clearly and unequivocally that it is *not* our intention, God forbid, to demean in any way the honor that is rightfully due parents. Not only is the practice of honoring parents a command of the Almighty, but they deserve it as well. In fact, every parent deserves more honor and esteem than children are capable of giving.

With that said, some practical parameters and limitations must be enforced in order to ensure the integrity and stability of your marriage. You have to give honor, that's true, and you *should* give it, plenty of it, for as long as your parents live — and after as well. That must never be an issue. *But* — be careful how your honor is expressed. An obligation to bestow endless amounts of honor is definitely *not* an invitation to a parent to meddle and interfere with the delicate internal machinery of a child's marriage and life.

Guided by halachah, determine what are appropriate expressions of honor; likewise determine what degree of deference and obedience is *outside* a parent's reasonable right to expect — and stay within those bounds.

You and your spouse founded your marriage on certain commonly shared ideals, and you run your home in accordance with those principles. Probably, those ideals generally correspond with the principles you were taught in your parents' homes. In other ways, the two of you have struck out on your own path in service of the *Ribono shel Olam*, in accordance with your vision of what He expects of you. However, regardless of how similar or dissimilar you and your parents' homes are, in matters of internal policy, ultimately only two people's votes count, and you know who those two people are.

Of course, you can solicit other people's advice, including that of your parents; in fact, you are encouraged to do so. Parents are usually glad to advise you and give you the benefit of their vast experience. Don't be quick to dismiss it. They have lived longer than you and have seen more than you have. They've "been there" — before you were born, in fact. They have made the mistakes that are an integral and indispensable part of learning and acquiring wisdom. So listen with an open and respectful mind. But take it for what it is — good solid advice, nothing more, nothing less. It's not a command or a decree.

Don't apologize or feel guilty for excluding your parents from the decision-making process; they don't belong. If your marriage is a healthy one, you and your spouse discuss major issues relating to matters of family policy. You consider yourselves partners — equal partners — and you are respectful and considerate of the opinions and wishes of your partner. No one else belongs in this inner circle with you, not children, nor friends, nor parents.

Here are some ideas to keep in mind:

1. Don't have disagreements in front of your parents.

Don't quarrel in front of your parents. It's too tempting, too inviting. They will jump into the fray. If you want to discuss some controversial, volatile family topic, do it after the big family barbecue has ended and the folks have gone home. Then, in the privacy of your own home, discuss the issue with your spouse — only.

2. Present a united front.

Present a united front to the outside world, even if, privately, the two of you don't agree with each other.

For example, suppose your parents ask you, "How long does he plan to sit and learn? When is he going to get a job and support his family?" You may wonder anxiously about that yourself, but don't tell that to them.

Answer loyally, something along the lines of, "We haven't made a final decision, yet." Don't let on or intimate that this is a sore point. You can disagree with your spouse, but do it in private.

3. Don't confide fights.

It may run counter to every instinct you have; it may fly in the face of your notion of what a parent (especially a mother) is all about. *But* — don't confide in your parent when you are having a fight with your spouse.

Why not?

If you are a wise disciple of the Tomer Devorah, when you are having a fight with your spouse, even a serious one, you remember nevertheless that the opponent squaring off against you is your beloved, the one you married, and, when all is said and done, your best friend. These considerations will, of course, temper your ferocity. Your mother and father don't share your sentiments in this regard. They may like your spouse, they may even love and respect him, but after all, *you* are their child, and they feel your pain, sometimes more intensely than you do.

Call your mother up, give her an earful of your complaints about your husband's callous and insensitive behavior, and hang up the phone. In an hour, perhaps a day, you'll forget about it, or the two of you will resolve your difference of opinion, or he, with a contrite and penitent heart, may even apologize and bring you a gift to symbolize his new resolve to atone for whatever misdeeds he may have committed. Whatever the case, long before you have gotten the phone bill for that conversation with your mom, the memory of the unpleasant incident that sparked your tirade will have faded from your mind.

But your mother may still recall every word, detail, and nuance of your discussion with her. She might have added to and embellished the story somewhere along the line, as she sits and broods over it for long hours stretching into days. And, on top of that, you usually don't call her up and tell her in the same graphic detail how you reconciled and worked every detail out. At some point in the future, when you're talking to your mother, she'll enquire grimly, "What's going to be with...?" and you'll laugh and dismiss it casually with a wave of your hand and a simple, "Oh, we worked it out." You might be a little surprised — and annoyed — to realize that your mother is still wrapped up with the past.

In fairness to your mother, it's not her fault. She loves you with the love that only a mother can feel for her child, and she suffers when you feel pain or anguish; add to this that *you* incited her — in excruciating detail — in your hour-and-a-half harangue, then reassured her in 2½ seconds without a substantive word. And, no matter how warmly and positively she may feel towards your husband, she doesn't — she can't — feel what you feel. Your anger is, by definition, tempered by the love you naturally feel for him. Your mother's anger has no such constraints on it. Her question reflects a simple fact:

while you got on with the business of living your life with your husband, and the fleeting bad feelings engendered by that negative experience have long since been replaced and overwhelmed by a steady stream of happy, pleasant shared times and interactions, your mother has had none of that positive interaction; she has been left to brood over the dark insight you gave her into your home and marriage. Can your casual dismissal and nonchalant wave of the hand put her restless mind at ease?

Have a similar conversation a couple of times a year for a few years, and your mother will — with ample justification — construct a composite picture of the unhappy life that her hapless daughter is forced to endure at the hands of her brutish husband, a picture that has, mercifully, little to do with reality. It's not fair to her, and it's not smart for you. She doesn't need the grief and the heartache, and you don't need the antipathy and resentment that will inevitably pit your mother against your husband, with (surprise!) you caught in the cross fire, a pawn in a deadly game of divide and conquer.

It's hard to extricate yourself from such a messy situation, so don't create one in the first place.

4. Ask advice on parve topics.

Give parents an outlet for sharing their wisdom. Make your parents — and in-laws — happy: ask them, unbidden, for advice. It'll make them feel great, and, who knows, you may actually learn something. But be careful to pick a topic that is sufficiently noncontroversial.

For some couples, asking any sort of advice from their parents has dangers and risks. Your folks may view this as an opportunity to overstep the boundaries that you set up and test for a response. What have they got to lose? Such forays into realms where they don't belong may lead to quarrels and feelings of resentment. So, if you can maintain tight controls on the process of asking your parents' advice, by all means go ahead. If you can't, and this is too tempting and slippery a slope, don't do it.

If you've gotten off to a rocky start with your in-laws, the following rules will help you recover:

5. Never speak against your in-laws.

Don't brag to the world that your in-laws are miserable people. There is nothing particularly romantic about the stereotype, and there is nothing to be proud of, either. By speaking in such a manner, you'll only reinforce and deepen whatever ill-will and animosity you may already feel for them (according to the Chovot Halevavot's insight that "*Machshevet hanefesh nimshach achar hadibbur*" — one's spirit is influenced by his speech).

If you happen to find yourself in a crowd of people who are sitting around and complaining about their in-laws, keep your mouth closed. Better yet, leave. This is really a "*moshav leitzim*" — session of scoffers,[15] and you have better things to do with your time than absorb

---

15. Tehillim 1:1.

their destructive attitudes.

Don't speak against your in-laws to your spouse, and don't insult them in his presence. Don't try to convince him what rotten people they are. Why would you want to? What can you possibly hope to accomplish? It's an unfair demand to make of your spouse that he be disloyal to his parents.

6. Be nice to your in-laws.

Be very nice to them, in fact. You owe them, after all. They gave birth to and raised your spouse, and, in fact, many of the fine qualities you admire in your spouse come directly from them. Whatever your in-laws do or say to you, you can't deny the great kindness they've done you. If they drive you more crazy than anyone else does, remember, they have also given you a greater gift than anyone else has. Silently repeat this to yourself a couple of hundred times as you pull into your in-laws' driveway.

If you cannot honestly feel anything for your in-laws, then, by all means, put on a good act. Be nice to them for your spouse's sake. It will give your spouse untold relief, happiness, and peace of mind. Strife between you and your in-laws invariably takes its toll and inspires no small amount of mental anguish in your spouse. Your spouse will recognize and appreciate any effort on your part to mitigate this tension. Don't tell your spouse that you're just acting, though. That is one secret that you shouldn't share.

One additional consideration should motivate you to

be nice to your in-laws. Chances are that if you are nice to your in-laws, your spouse will be nice to your parents. Wouldn't that be nice?

For Wives

1. Build your husband's self-esteem.

Show your husband plenty of respect; do whatever you can to build his self-esteem. He might seem to be a big tough bully on the outside; in fact, inside he is probably a scared little boy.

And, of course, the more respect you show him, the more you will feel towards him.

Concentrate on areas in which your husband excels (e.g., learning, professional success, kindness/charity, etc.) rather than areas in which he needs work (e.g., helping around the house, relating to the children or in-laws, etc.).

2. Don't be a tzaddeket at your family's expense.[16]

The rule of thumb is anything you can do to reduce the amount of stress in the house, do. Stress is the great enemy of marital harmony and tranquility.

For example, your enormous responsibilities to home and family leave you with precious little time as it is. Don't increase the amount of stress in your house by spreading yourself too thin and committing yourself, say,

---

16. Based on R. Yisrael Salanter's advice.

to too many projects outside the house. Budget your time and prioritize your obligations and enterprises. If activities outside the home bring stress *into* your home, curtail them abruptly.

Sure, we all know super women who, besides raising twelve perfect tzaddikim ages one to twelve while maintaining a calm, immaculate home, volunteer what seems to be endless amounts of time and energy to their shul's chessed committee, the local *bikur cholim*, and the women's league, and cook for and entertain half-a-dozen newly observant singles in their home every Shabbat, all effortlessly. If you can't do this without driving yourself and your family crazy, don't. And don't feel guilty about it, either. In the time that is left to you after you have fulfilled your familial obligations, do what you comfortably can to improve yourself and perform acts of kindness and charity.

For Husbands

1. Make your wife happy.

The Torah commands a husband to make his wife happy. Most commentators understand this command to refer to the first year of marriage especially. At least one commentator, though, understands this command to apply equally always, throughout all the years of marriage. The halachah is determined by the majority view, but the minority opinion supplies us with a philosophy and an attitude that should animate your marriage at all times.

A woman's nature is to work for her household. Her gaze and attention are focused naturally on her family and home. She works diligently on behalf of her husband and children.

However, whether those tasks are performed with happiness or, *ch"v*, with resentment depends on the husband and his recognition of and reciprocation for her contributions to the family. The wife's feelings, in turn, set the general tone of the home.

Therefore, if you want a happy, content home, do everything you can to make your wife happy and content. A happy wife is the greatest resource you can have.

2. Respect your wife's intelligence.

> "...*V'al tarbeh sichah im ha'ishah*" — Do not chat too much with your wife (*Pirkei Avot* 1:5).

This mishnah in *Pirkei Avot* immediately follows the mishnah which exhorts us to associate with and learn from the sages of the generation. Why are these two mishnayot placed in such close proximity? The answer is based on the use of the word "*sichah*" (chatter) with regard to the exchange between husband and wife. After spending the day outside the house learning and discussing important, meaningful Torah ideas with your fellows and teachers, don't come home and talk nonsense to your wife. Don't reserve your mindless chatter for your wife. She deserves more and is capable of more, so give her more. Don't exclude her from your life outside the house.[17]

3. Don't be a tzaddik at your family's expense.[18]

Your personal righteousness is worthless (in fact, it's the opposite of righteousness) when it is acquired or practiced at the expense of your wife's or children's legitimate needs (e.g., psychological, emotional, etc.).

Consider the following example. I happened to observe a certain *kollel* family once. The husband has something of a reputation as a promising *talmid chacham. He is a quiet young man, but very outspoken in his humility. "I'm an am ha'aretz* (ignoramus)," he bemoans sincerely in conversation every once in a while. Those who hear his proclamations admire his great humility, but I noticed that his words have a markedly different effect on his wife. They devastate her.

His wife is a heroic woman in her unassuming way. Besides raising a large family and keeping a quiet, orderly home, she struggles to support the family financially and emotionally and to fill the void caused by her husband's absence due to long hours of study. She comforts herself with the consolation that the privation and struggle she endures is worthwhile if her husband is able to learn undistracted and becomes a great *talmid chacham*. In this case, his outspoken declarations of humility, be-

---

17. Based on the explanation of R. Hirsch.
18. Based on R. Yisrael Salanter's advice.

cause they take a mental and emotional toll on his wife, are not worth very much.

Don't volunteer excessive amounts of time outside the house when you are sorely needed by your wife and children at home. There are plenty of opportunities to perform mitzvot in your own home; take care of these before you go looking for extra mitzvah opportunities outside your house. Neglecting the homemade variety in favor of outside mitzvah opportunities may indicate that your interest isn't just in performing mitzvot.

4. Follow R. Chiya's example.[19]

R. Chiya's wife was well known for not being the easiest woman to live with, nor the most agreeable. Nevertheless, whenever R. Chiya found a gift that his wife would like, he would bring it home for her in recognition and appreciation of the many blessings she provided for him.

Bring your wife gifts. The size of the gift doesn't matter. What matters is that you bring gifts home often, whenever you can. For maximum effect, wrap your gift in a pretty box and present it with some ceremony.

5. Never compliment another woman's appearance.

All women are somewhat sensitive or insecure about their appearance. In this world of glamour women, most wives imagine there is somebody around whom their

---

19. *Yevamot* 63a.

husband fancies more attractive. Make your wife feel she is the most beautiful woman in the world to you; nobody could possibly compete. (You will come to believe it, if you say it enough times.)

6. Respect your wife's feminine attitudes and characteristics.

You are a man. Your wife, however, is *not* a man; don't try to make her one.

Don't belittle or dismiss the uniquely feminine attitudes your wife possesses (e.g., her regard for the aesthetic, etc.), some of the very qualities that attracted you to her in the first place.

You might wonder (with some exasperation) why your wife insists that you serve the rice at Shabbat dinner in a pretty dish rather than straight from the pot, even when no company is around. In her eyes, the infusion of beauty and elegance into the home is neither unnecessary, frivolous, nor wasteful.

Stacking the Deck In Your Favor

1. Ask the Almighty to help you.

Beg the Almighty to assist you in your holy campaign to improve your marriage and yourself. Health, longevity, marital harmony, material prosperity, and progeny are all His department. Don't be afraid to ask Him to help you.

" 'For *this* shall every righteous person pray
to You....' What's 'this'? R. Chanina said: A
good wife" (*Berachot* 8a).

2. Get yourself a good Rav.

Find a Rav whom you can trust, in whom you can
confide, and to whom you can turn for advice. In addition to halachic credentials, he should possess compas-
sion, sensitivity, and insight in generous amounts.

Don't just ask him if that *fleishig* pot in which you
accidently cooked your *milchig* supper is still kosher. Ask
him about marriage and childrearing, too. The Torah
addresses all of these issues. No aspect of the human
experience is outside the purview of Torah. There is
much more to Judaism than the "ritual" aspects. Find a
Rav who will introduce you to the rest of the Torah's
wisdom.

6

CONCLUSION

WHILE OUR TOPIC is by no means exhausted, the information and ideas presented here should form the basis for a regiment of improving your marriage, as well as enhancing your general ability to interact successfully with people (including yourself).

The Chovot Halevavot writes, "The days are like notebooks — write in them that which you want remembered about you."[20] Someday, after 120 years, we are all going to die. Ask yourself a few simple, sobering questions: How will you be remembered? How do you *want* to be remembered? How do you want your children to remember you? Your husband or wife? Your neighbors, friends, and coworkers?

Every day of your life, while you interact with the

---

20. *Shaar Cheshbon Hanefesh* 3:11.

people around you, you create the image they have of you, the image of you that they will carry with them long after you've departed this world for the next.

Look, for a moment, at the children playing at your feet. Someday you won't be with them anymore, and they will have many occasions (during *Yizkor*, on *Yahrtzeits*, at *Sedarim* and other family events, or when their great-grandchildren ask them about you) to conjure up the images and recollections of you that *you* "wrote" in the "notebooks" of their minds and hearts. What would you like to record in their durable albums? Don't leave such an important decision to happenstance. Decide. Then actively start filling up their "notebooks" with the best pictures of yourself that you can produce.

The same goes for your spouse. He is every bit as diligent and faithful in recording the pictures of you that will endure for eternity.

And how are *you* going to remember yourself and your performance as husband or wife, parent, and Jew? You will have ample opportunity in the twilight of your life — and beyond — to evaluate how faithfully you executed the duties and responsibilities the Almighty gave you when He gave you life in this world. Will it be with great pride and satisfaction, or, *ch"v*, with shame and recrimination?

Hakadosh Baruch Hu does not give us challenges that we can't pass "with flying colors."

"The Almighty does not overburden His

creatures" (*Avodah Zarah* 3a).

"When Hashem knows that a righteous person can and will do His will, and He desires to make him an even greater person, he sends challenges to that person; He does not provide such challenges to the wicked who will not listen [and, therefore, fail]" (Ramban, Bereishit 22:1).

If He set up the rules of this game, then there must be a way for us to win. There is. Resolve that you *will* win. Begin today — right now, in fact — putting into practice some of the Torah-insights you have learned. Take the first tentative steps, and the Almighty will give wings to your feet. You have His promise.

"On the way in which a person wants to go, he is led [by the Almighty]" (*Makkot* 10b).

"Open for Me an opening the size of a needle's eye, and I will open for you an opening the size of the gates of the Holy Temple" (see *Shir Hashirim Rabbah*, beg. of ch. 5).

The Rambam in his commentary on *Pirkei Avot* observes that "whatever level a person is on when he dies — *thus will he remain for all eternity.*" See to it that your eternal level is an astonishingly high one. It is a worthy prize that beckons, and your spouse can be invaluable in helping you attain it.

If you have already made every mistake described in this book, don't despair. Keep reminding yourself of the famous story about R. Yisrael Salanter's encounter with the cobbler:

R. Yisrael once entered the workshop of a cobbler with a pair of shoes that needed repair. He observed the man hard at work and also noted the gathering dusk that encroached on the shop. The darkness was held at bay only by the short stub of what had once been a tallow candle as it struggled to retain its tenuous grasp on a tiny, flickering flame. The feeble light played unpredictably over the man's hands as he worked.

"Leave them," the cobbler instructed and gestured to a spot where R. Yisrael could put his shoes. "I'll work on them next, in a little while."

R. Yisrael was skeptical as he surveyed the scene. "I can come back tomorrow, if you would prefer," he offered.

"No, no," the cobbler shook his head. "*Kol zeman di lichtele brent,*" he explained, "*me ken farrichten.*" As long as the candle burns, one can still repair.

R. Yisrael was electrified by the man's words. The shoes were forgotten for the moment — the man had given him, and all of *Klal Yisrael,* a much greater gift. Whatever has been in the past, as long as you live, as long as the Almighty mercifully deigns to continue giving you His most precious gift and "*di lichtele brent,*" get busy repairing: your relationships with your spouse, with other people, with yourself, and with the Almighty. Don't waste time bemoaning the past; get busy fixing for the future.